SOMEONE ELSE'S LIFE

Kapka Kassabova is a cross-genre writer with a special interest in deep journeying, exploring human geographies, and the hidden narratives of places, people, and peripheries. She has published two poetry collections with Bloodaxe, *Someone else's life* (2003) and *Geography for the Lost* (2007). Born in 1973 in Sofia, Bulgaria, she emigrated to New Zealand with her family in 1992, where published two poetry collections, *All roads lead to the sea* and *Dismemberment* (Auckland University Press), and two novels, *Reconnaissance* and *Love in the Land of Midas* (Penguin NZ).

In 2005 she moved to Edinburgh, Scotland, and wrote *Street Without a Name* (Granta, 2008), a coming-of-age story set in the twilight years of totalitarian Communism, shortlisted for the Prix Européen du Livre and the Stanford-Dolman Travel Book Awards. Her memoir-history, *Twelve Minutes of Love* (Granta, 2011), blends a tale of obsession and migration with a history of the Argentine tango, and was shortlisted for the Scottish Mortgage Investment Book Awards. *Villa Pacifica* (Alma Books 2011), a novel with an Ecuadorian setting, came out at the same time.

Border: a journey to the edge of Europe (Granta/Graywolf, 2017) explores the remote triple borderlands of Bulgaria, Turkey and Greece where the easternmost stretch of the Iron Curtain ran. Described by the British Academy Prize jury as 'being about the essence of place and the essence of human encounter', its narratives weave into a panoramic study of how borderlines shape human destiny through time. *Border* won the British Academy's Al-Rodhan Prize for Global Cultural Understanding, the Saltire Scottish Book of the Year, the Edward Stanford-Dolman Travel Book of the Year, and the inaugural Highlands Book Prize. It was shortlisted for the Baillie-Gifford Prize, the Bread and Roses Prize, the Duff Cooper Prize, the Royal Society of Literature Ondaatje Prize, the National Book Critics Circle Awards (USA), and the Gordon Burn Prize.

Kapka Kassabova lives in the Highlands of Scotland. She is a juror for the Neustadt Prize (2019-2020), and was on the judging panel for the International Dublin Book Award (2017). Her next book is *To the Lake: a Balkan journey of war and peace* (Granta/Graywolf 2020).

KAPKA KASSABOVA

Someone else's life

BLODAXE BOOKS

Copyright © Kapka Kassabova 1997, 1998, 2003

ISBN: 978 1 85224 617 4

First published 2003 by
Bloodaxe Books Ltd,
Eastburn,
South Park,
Hexham,
Northumberland NE46 1BS.

This is a digital reprint of the 2003 edition.

www.bloodaxebooks.com

For further information about Bloodaxe titles
please visit our website and join our mailing list
or write to the above address for a catalogue.

Supported using public funding by
**ARTS COUNCIL
ENGLAND**

Cover design: Neil Astley & Pamela Robertson-Pearce.

Printed in Great Britain by
www.Printondemand-worldwide.com, Peterborough.

for my parents

Acknowledgements

The last two sections of this book are poems published in earlier versions in Kapka Kassabova's collections, *All roads lead to the sea* (1997) and *Dismemberment* (1998), both published in New Zealand by Auckland University Press.

Acknowledgements are due to the following New Zealand and Australian publications where some of these poems first appeared: *Glottis, HEAT, Landfall, Poetry New Zealand, Sport* and *Trout*. Some were included in *Parallel Histories*, an installation in collaboration with Nancy de Freitas at Auckland's Fisher Gallery.

Contents

DISMEMBERMENT

ALL ROADS LEAD TO THE SEA:
young poems from the end of the world

PLACE

Place

This is why we come

To wake up to the crowing of plucked roosters
from a sepia childhood

To watch the merging of dawn and dusk,
as matter-of-fact as a lesson in evanescence.

To see without a warning white herons in the bay
still with rarity, guarding their reflection.

To spot a hooded figure on the hill in a yellow raincoat,
in a flashback of self-recognition.

To lie, then stand and fall into the deep storm
from a great height, emerging on the other side of here.

To sleep and when you wake up, to remember it
as something that did not exist, and that will never be again.

This is why we leave.

My Life in Two Parts

1

Outside my window is a row of poplars
growing from the turf of childhood.
Poplars grow in rows, never on their own.
It is Christmas. The sky is full of stars,
the branches are bare,
the wolves distant and menacing.
Now is the only time for oranges.
Their brisk fragrance fills the nails
as we lie in cold rooms high in the Balkans
dreaming of palm trees and the world.

2

Outside my window is a palm tree.
It is winter. The sky is enormous
and the ocean follows the moon.
Oranges are on the window-sill with other
tropical fruit no longer of interest.
Bright-plumed parakeets sway in the palm tree
and that's the only time I look up.
I lie in the low, stuffy rooms of adulthood
dreaming of poplars and the world.
Always, they come in rows.

In the Shadow of the Bridge

Wherever we went, something else
was on our minds.
It was too hot, it was too cold.
We were tired, we were not in the mood.
We had been there. It wasn't what we wanted.
We were the constant witnesses of ourselves.

One evening, the moon rose from the horizon
like we'd never seen it:
enormous and yellow.
We drove towards it in the falling night.
We knew it was a rare chance.

We stopped at the roots of a bridge.
We stood in its giant shadow,
pierced by the headlights of passing cars above.
Across the black, wind-combed water was a city
and all its alien lights. We had come from that city.
Your camera on a tripod by the edge of the water.
I sat inside the vintage car.
The moon bulged right above us.

We had everything that night.
So we took a picture and drove away.

Angel's Lament

(for Gail)

I'm looking down into a valley of vapours
where yet another city lies, concealed
and dense with lives I've seen
that have not seen me
for I am citizen of the unknown

All my life, I have wanted this:
to be inside the story
to have a street with a name and a corner shop
to have a window with curtains
and all the sharp noises of the night
in some city wedged in between mountains
in some city carpeted with ocean

To know that I've arrived
to be concealed from the terrible
longing of some stranger
who will come one day
and stand on top of the mountain, unseen
then vanish, leaving footprints in the air

Immigrant Architectures

These days, you feel uneasy
about closing your eyes.
You are afraid of finding

your native city so familiar
and so aloof
you'll wonder if you've really
been there.

You'll find yourself
sitting inside a distant season
quivering every now and then
like a cheese in brine.

You'll find the restored
front of a palace
and behind it
the ruins of your neighbourhood.

Boulevards paved
with familiar faces
watch you and cry out
in a chorus of displeasure.

All-embracing loves
close in on nothing,
like dancing with yourself.

And the sea, the sepia sea
inside your glass head
that everybody sees
and no one understands.

And what you've known mutates.
And what you've known
is something else,

something like the shadow
of a predatory bird gliding
into the great stillness
before a great storm

which is only the storm
of your blood
in the cracked cup of memory.

Amnesia at Eaglereach

It was the hour of sudden chills.
I woke up and I was standing
in a room on top of a mountain.

Vapours filled the valley below
concealing its depth –
a white Styx that travelled slowly
between here and somewhere else.

I needed to remember.
But the trees stood in the still air,
their sharp leaves betraying nothing.

Small animals with names I didn't know
scurried on the roof
and a rain of pebbles fell.
'Listen,' I said. I turned around.

Then I remembered:
there had never
been anyone.

The Pied Piper of Buenos Aires
(for Richard)

In the city of cupolas
and holes in the pavement
a man crossed the street, carefully.
He wore an unfamiliar shirt.
It must have been summer.
The city lived its last dream of glory.
His steps were unhurried, the future was distant.
His mind was filled with thoughts
I cannot read because
I didn't know him.

Now, bats come out of the cupolas at night
and fill the low sky with whispers.
Children rummage through rubbish bags
and the homeless with their dogs
sleep obliquely on the subway steps.
I see a man in a familiar white shirt
crossing the street without looking.
I wave to him from my crumbling balcony
but it is dark. Trees have grown in the way.
I know him but he walks

like the Pied Piper without looking back.

One Sunday in New Zealand

One Sunday in New Zealand,
everything was out of reach,
inexplicable and vague in the distance.

A family of Russians strolled past,
the old man in checkered trousers,
the women blonde and the BMW
gleaming as they drove away.

An alcoholic in a tatty coat
stood facing the ocean,
an empty space beside him where
a dog had been or a woman.

We walked down the jetty
to the lighthouse, and after what seemed
many hours of wind, we were greeted
by mute Asians with fishing rods.

And the ocean, all of it.
The volcanic island of Rangitoto
lay symmetrically in the mist.
We watched the waves lapping at nothing.

Do you think our lives
will be like this from now on?
I turned to ask.
But you already knew, you took my hand

and we started walking back towards the land
where nothing is ours and so
nothing is ever the same.

Watching a man fail to drown himself

I saw you
You came to the beach as you did at the end
Of each day, to hide in the water
To pretend you were leaving
To return to the shore
(your head lonely and comical like a pea in soup)
As if from a new place

But that day there was something different
About the way you unstrapped your watch
As if it were clinging to you
The way you took off your T-shirt
As if you'd borrowed it
The way you stepped on the sharp deposit of shells
As if they didn't cut your feet

You waded in as you did at the end of each day
But that day for some reason
The tide was out and as your legs pushed forward
With mounting panic, seeking depth
I knew how you felt:
Even the sea had betrayed you

Now you would walk across to the island
Then walk back, the water beating
Against your angry knees
You would find your clothes untouched
You had really nowhere to go
Nowhere to return from

Nature morte

At midnight, in the narrow mirror
I see a figure
perched on the edge of the bed.
Behind, another figure, stretched out,
sleeping or worse – silent.
Luckily, their faces are lost in darkness.

The room is full of flowers, the air
rotting with fragrance.
Today is my birthday. We remain as we are
but nothing can stop us –
we are falling
like fruit from a midnight tree.

If the morning comes
rose petals would cover the floor.
We would be genuinely surprised:
so this is how long things of beauty last.
This is how much can happen
in a single night.

The complete circle

I am afraid of being alone
with your body in the night.
I am afraid to bear witness
to your sleep.
As if it's a puzzle in need of a solution
instead of a solution in itself.

In your damp embrace, I sleep to forget you.

*

I dream of gutted, lit-up buildings
in troubled cities of the world
that are everywhere and nowhere.
It is twilight,
I am looking for a place to live.
Dogs watch from the shadows.

I wake up homeless.

*

Before me, leaf-light curtains,
the moon looking sharply down.
Behind me, your uneven breath.
Your arms, unslackened by sleep
encircle me.
The night will never end and I am grateful.

I am grateful and I am still afraid.

*

Later in the night I understand:
there is no solution. This
is the beginning and the end in one.
The home with the light always on
and the gutted house with the dogs waiting.
There is nowhere else.

Your arms are the complete circle.

Balinese

One: taking a photograph

This is the Indian ocean,
breaking white over sharp coral.
When the tide is out
fishermen wade in and stand
with their backs to the island all day.
They have gone now,
everyone has gone.
The outlines of dogs
guard the gates of the night.
Out in the empty field
behind luxury hotels
garbage flutters,
white blossoms fall from trees
with nobody to stand beneath,
smiling photogenically
so the filth, the heat
and the absence of hope
become exotic backdrop.
Tonight, I am the backdrop.
I am the blurry stranger in the photograph,
with her mouth open almost in laughter,
saying: This is not my ocean.
This is not my pain.

Two: Made

In my false luxury hotel
I think of you tonight, Made –
second child with no father,
taken out of school at just eleven
when the money ran out.
Made from the village in the north
where nobody goes
and your mother sits
in the eternal shade
waiting for your letter,
nodding to mountain ghosts.

You have left the café of Bali Sun
where it's always sunset
at the end of a long, empty evening
sick from the blare of MTV
and the copper shine of tourists.
For us you smiled and spoke
your self-taught English.
For us you were the friendly local.

You have taken off your apron,
wiped off your smile
and walked to your room.
You have washed your clothes
ready for tomorrow,
lit a cigarette and lain
in the humid night.
You listen to the ocean
break over the reef.
You think of me and my white tribes,
how your life is our holiday.
We're out of here tomorrow but you,
you're only twenty four
and you don't dare dream
before you go to sleep.

Indian Story

This is day one of a new waiting
which is an old waiting
unmeasured by days.

The man with crutches
at the traffic-lights
is waiting
for the storm to lift
his single footprint
from the dust
and carry it elsewhere.
The storm comes.
Dust covers the footprint.
Nobody moves.
Nothing will change.

This
is the measure of the day.

Berlin – Mitte

I live in a haunted house.
I have lost my hunger. I have lost my sleep.
When I sleep, my dreams are not mine.

My sense of time is unstable
and I wait for anonymous
midnight visits. I feel that all
that is to come is inevitable.

I have my suitcase close-by, but it's empty –
I know I'll be surprised. I'm ready
to leave my possessions behind.

I look for clues around the house.
But the walls are white-washed.
The ceilings are too high.
The floor has been treated with the polish
of this new, confident century.

I sit by the narrow window remembering
those I never knew,
for there is no one to remember them.
No one remembers numbers on a plaque.

I fear they will come one night,
after sixty years of absence.
I will offer them the house of course, the bed,
the kitchen table, but I fear they will say
that what was taken from them
can never be given back.

Someone else's life

It was a day of slow fever
and roses in the doorway, wrapped
in yesterday's news of death.

Snow fell like angels' feathers
from a dark new sky, softly announcing
that some things would never be the same.

I listened carefully to doubts and revisions
of someone else's life, safe in my room of tomorrow,
a passing witness to sorrow and wonder.

Then night came and I was quickly
drifting inside that life. I was leaving mine.
Snowflakes continued to fall.

The street was deserted and dim.
Shrapnel wounds blossomed in stone walls.
There was no proof of the current decade,

and I could not recall
the names of faces that I knew
the smell of places where I'd lived

and why I lay alone now
so close to a vast, empty floor, so far
from the sun, so far.

Looking for Lieselotte Stein

At the junk market on Sunday
lying at the bottom of a plastic crate,
I found the book of destiny.
It belonged to Lieselotte Stein
in 1931. Her school-mates wrote
a poem each, 'in everlasting memory'.

I went looking for her, I went
inside the darkest courtyards
at the heart of Berlin winter.
I heard the shuffle of dim lives
inside naked windows, I opened gates
heavy with unuse.
I stood in cold arches
under dripping railways.
I crossed bridges with no names
over empty boats drifting on the river.
I moved inside the fog
of this new century, the sky so hard and low
I could close it like a lid over my head.

When I danced closely with strangers
in dim hallways, I thought
of Lieselotte Stein red-lipped in furs,
betraying her beloved with the strong of the day.
When I fell to my knees I wondered
if Lieselotte stood up for anything.
When I stood dwarfed by the buildings of her city,
I saw Lieselotte, small and lost
among the ruins of her house.

Finally, I found the address of Lieselotte Stein.
My hand shook over the doorbell.
When she opened the door,
I handed over the notebook.

I said my name, the current decade
and gave my reasons for being.
But she croaked: 'Go away.
I've settled my accounts with destiny.
Can't you see: I don't exist.'

Railway dream

One night on the railway,
a girl slept, or someone slept
who looked like her.

In the middle of her sleep, a train passed
first in a flash,
then slowing down to a rattle:
the Yesterday Express.

In the train slept a conductor
in a shivery blue shirt
with eyes of fever
a voice like an ashtray
and a string of worry-beads.

In the middle of his dream
he saw borders
between one dark side and another

He saw red peppers on strings
against whitewash

Dogs with an odd number of legs

Children waving at the train
before throwing stones,
then firing guns

Old men chewing old poisons,
grinning gaps instead of smiles

In valleys strewn with garbage and roses
in fields where vines and fires soared

And somewhere on the railway
he saw a girl standing
with her suitcase.

He tried to stop the train
but it wasn't moving.
She tried to wake up
but she was wide-awake.

That's how they never met.

The Crescendo

It isn't so much a place
as a colour.
Not so much a colour
as a persistence.
Not so much a colour
as a mud-brown fear
that won't go away.

It falls like smog
over the cherished ecology
of the moment.
It rises in small nauseating puffs
like a subterranean sewage-city.
It gurgles in the Harbour
like a shock-wave
from distant carnage.
It whispers horrors of tenderness.
It slithers towards you
though it's not alive.
It shrinks away
like the mercurial future.

And somewhere in the middle of this
an Italian aria swells the air
with tragic bosomfuls
of unrequited love.

War has a special crescendo
for those who are there to hear.

In transit

There is a field of frozen mud
and in the middle – a border.
On this side of the border
a pear tree that doesn't bear fruit.
Under the tree an old man
in a borrowed jacket
with a plastic bag,
sitting or kneeling
against the trunk.
The mud has embraced his movements.
The others have gone on with their children.

The border is ten steps away.

Refugees

Look: the poverty of rain
Let's gather it in thimbles of patience
then pour it out in the mud

Meanwhile
we'll count all the worlds
to which we'll never go

We must remember – memory is hope.
But quietly, for words can cut out gaps in us
so wide we'd find
too many bodies lying there

Forget, we must forget
the memories – they open up and blossom
like switch-blades in the guts

Look: this is the world we have
Too poor to hide in
Too dark to cross, too single to forget

The Pacific seen from above

Here in the iron white sky
we move against the day, we are constantly
somewhere between Monday and Tuesday.
We move like death's shadow.

The people we know are far away
and we sit squeezed among strangers,
gazing down where the oceans of the world
are hard and open like graves.

Will we die our separate,
unknown deaths one day?
Or together, now – thrown
into sudden intimacy.

We eat our plastic breakfast and read
in yesterday's paper how
a visual artist awaits
the next man-made disaster.

She says they are always
extremely beautiful.

GATE TO ALL YOUR FAREWELLS

Cicadas

It was an impervious summer

The cicadas came out after
their immeasurable hibernation
Mated for twenty four hours
and died with great ferocity

We found them along the path
Their wings elaborate and hard
Their bellies iridescent
Their death abrupt and glorious

We fed them to the stone-patient trout
then fished the trout and ate it
It was delicious to the sound of cicadas
It filled us with a slow fear

We knew the summer was over
when the earth pulled us, when a brown
damp sky closed over us
and we wished to be like them

Lemon Tree Witnessing Man Being Built In

No, I said
as I stood between the house to be
and the house to die. You mustn't.
Anyway the opposite of memory
takes over in the end. Believe me.
I am a tree.

You were too tired to speak.
You just pointed with your chin
to the large, blurred architectures of the past
that explain your urge for demolition.
The old story I knew.

You loved a woman, and she loved you.
You lived in the house.
Many years passed.
It wasn't going to change.
But it changed.
You loved the memory of her
and missed her terribly.

You fed some chickens and grew some forests
around the house
and missed her terribly.
You left and travelled the world
which was empty of her.
You returned.
You read some books on relevant topics.
You aged. She aged without you.
You missed her terribly.

Until one day you said Right.
That's enough.
You made a decision about the house.
One needs more comfort, you explained
though I was merely a witness.
One needs a new house. The old house must go.

Wait a moment, I said
standing in the way as I always had.
By pulling the house down
you won't forget.
Whatever you do, you won't forget.
Believe me. I am a tree.

But you were beyond reasoning.
You just pointed with your chin
to the builders who came
in their trucks and T-shirts
and started laying bricks and mortar.
They covered you up to your neck in no time.

Before your calm face disappeared
I saw reflected in your eyes
the rubble of the old house.
I saw a terrible absence.
And bitterly, I shed a small sun.
It rolled down to your feet.
Here, for the new house.
For the long, dark centuries of happiness.

Two Nights

1 *Night of electrical storm*

The night was multiple. It couldn't possibly end.

Electricity – the quick outline of a wild animal –
jumped from house to sky and then
to a third and stranger place beyond our senses.

When the noise thinned down I knew:
the rain had hidden in the waterfall above.
You were sad. You love rain on the roof.

The room filled with a select crowd:
cripples from the past, supermen from the future
icon-faced lessons with disapproving lips.

We were suddenly among chipped shadows.
We tried to remain whole by lying very still
and thinking of nothing.

From that third and stranger place
we were being watched with pity.
(The place was later found to be Memory.)

When the night ended, it was like the end of an era.

2 *Night of poverty*

After the multiple night came the single night.
In the single night there was

a single window and in it
a single outline of a mountain
a single star above the mountain

a watch pushing single-handedly
each moment
towards the window's edge.

And not a single shadow
Not a single memory.
Not a single hope.

Yet it was no different from other nights.
It was the same window, mountain, star.
Even the waterfall was there, minimally.

We were no different from ourselves.
You – sleeping aridly like a desert
where I pitched my Bedouin tent.
And I – with my worry beads, not minding.

Really there was no reason why
poverty spilled its gentle acid over that night,
burning the beginning into the end.

No reason why we found
a beggar's dawn so full of holes
there was nothing left of it.

Embracing the umbrella

Once, I lived under an umbrella for four seasons.
It was large, white and on windy days
it revolved slowly to the left as if tilting
its head in a question.

The first season, I hid from the rain,
waiting for the sun.
The second season, I hid from the sun,
waiting for the rain.

The third, I waited for one
of the many clouds passing over
to stop for me. Waiting took up
the best of the last season too.

By then, I was trying
to pull the umbrella down –
it had become my prison.
But it wouldn't fall.

I tried to uproot it and take it with me –
it had become all I had.
But it was welded to the ground.

I tried to climb on top of it –
it had become my roof.
I managed that. I surveyed the day.

And I saw clearly:
there was nothing else but
this umbrella. Nothing
worth leaving for.

And so I stayed.

Twelve ways to photograph white lilies

1

In the antechamber I sit in a chair
that creaks every time
I turn to see if it's the door creaking
opening to the touch of your knee.

Outside, the field I crossed to come here
has been flooded by the angry sea I sailed
to come here. Only the sky has been spared.
But I didn't fly here.

In the kitchen, you are watering white lilies
seeking relief from the question
that darkens the day like a bird's shadow
passing over an empty road.

In the bedroom cold white sheets
like blank pages of books
wait for you to return, alone
and hold them against your face

and find the answer to that question about
the unguarded moment of love
and what comes after.

2

It is always in the late evening that hope crumbles
and something else takes over

Always to the record of some Portuguese chanteuse
to the smell of roast dinner
to the flicker of candles and the glimmer of gold wine

Always under the distant, sardonic stars that reduce
doubt to mere eternity

In the midst of such rustic beauty
how can I pound my rage
against resin-smelling doors?

Over dinner, you will talk about twelve ways
to photograph white lilies

You will remain on your side of silence or chatter
Crossing over to mine is crossing a wild river

I will mention leaving but you will quietly remind me
there are no boats or planes or open roads
at this hour of the night

It never entered my mind

It is a Miles Davis blues
they must have heard before.

She says,

It reminds me of October rain
on a New York roof past midnight.

A trumpet player in the Paris Métro
with a hole in his knee and eyes of fever.

A winter in the south – any south
among perched villages and wailing winds.

Anybody's childhood in an East European city
of shadows and fog.

A galaxy of dim bars along the street
in Berlin of the thirties.

The silver rustle of a single noun
yet to be coined, to mean complete sadness.

Railway stations in pre-war Italy
with snow-peaks in the crisp distance.

Lovers in worn-out coats
standing in the rain...

That's nice, he says,
except you've never left this town.

She says, my love, it reminds me of the day
when you and I will part.

How to survive in the desert

I cannot be lonely, I am a desert
DAVID HOWARD

Once I opened my door and a desert
drifted in, the most beautiful I had seen:
mellow, rippling with mirages

I entered it
It whispered to me storms of sand
It stroked my future with its whiteness

It sang to me from afar, it retreated
It undulated and sighed
at the crumbling edges of my thirst

Until there was nothing left
not even a small cactus or a passing cloud

I had gone too far to return
I couldn't advance any more
The sand had drunk the water of my days

Desert, I whispered, I offer myself to you
I lay down and waited
But the desert would not take me or let me go

Time passed away
The weather stopped
Nothing remained and yet nothing was over

Until I understood
There was only one way now

I had to become the desert
To lie, to sleep, to hum
To never want again

The Secret

I didn't know why
the day was sudden and the sky menacing.
Pink blossoms fell from trees,
covered the ground and rotted at once.
The rooster's crowing pierced our sleeps
which were separate.
All night, we hadn't touched.

You climbed a tree.
I hoped that you would scream and fall.
But you took a pair of pruning scissors and cut
a branch of blossoms. You couldn't stand
to watch them fall so pink still,
so full of life, you might have said.
But you said nothing. For hours, you said nothing.

The seasons passed through me.
I saw what had been clear for some time.
And you – you had always known why.

How we make love

Every time you lie down
it is a last surrender:
the flesh falls away from your face
revealing someone else.
Your hands alight on top of your body.
Your ribs smile sadly at the ceiling.

Every time you lie down
it is a last invitation.
So I stand by the window
and together, we see a green place
with no end, with no name,
where this will be a memory.

The Hour of Giving Up

While you were away
I was lying here
amidst the ruins of the moon,
inside the humming of the ocean,
the heavy sky leaning against tall
unbroken windows.
I was waiting.

And the hour I feared has come,
the hour when you've arrived
and yet you aren't here,
the hour of dark hills and flies trapped
inside the double glazing,
the tide leaving thick veins of mud behind,
and you reading next door, or sleeping.

I'm still waiting, the summer has been
and gone. You don't come into my room.
And as you get up and move
around the creaky house, whistling
I see that you will never be here.
That you do not exist.
That I must give up what I've waited for.

The Crossing

The ropes uncoil, boards creak beneath me.
This is the last boat of the day.
You flap your arms
as if about to take off.

I look up – in the sky
there is an opening of fire.
I look back – you remain
unmoving, on your barren island.

I flap my arms, this is my last attempt.
My shoes fall off,
damp cloud tugs at me,
I try to step inside the opening.

But the sky is not a doorway.
Fire is an illusion of the dying day.
And neither this nor the absence of it
is an answer.

The room, the field

In a room you'll never see I lie
listening to wallpaper peeling.

When we are most in pain, you said once,
we must put things in perspective.

And so the room becomes a flower
with slowly curling petals.

The flower is in a field which is the time
we have left to remember and feel.

In a room I've seen, you stand
talking to chickens, folding handkerchiefs.

When winter comes, the field turns yellow and shrinks.
You wait. Winter comes. It isn't true.
You remember and feel everything.

Gate to All Your Farewells

1

Stop moving towards me
Still your breath
Spread your heart evenly
so that it won't break

Enter the forest of my farewells
Your steps will be muffled
Your hands brushing
the warmth of bark

Sit under a tree of your choice
and close your eyes
I am here
You have arrived

2

Now that she is gone again
And again, forever

Who will close your day
With lips of silence

Who will listen to the waterfall at night
When nothing else is real

Who will peel the bark with patient fingers
And collect the resin of your heart

Who will light the candles
Who will blow them out

I will
Unmoving shadow by the fire

Breath on glass, feather of voice
Face of illusion

Gate to all your farewells
I will

DISMEMBERMENT

Calculations

The fire that lights a candle
cannot be shared between the wick
and the match, it has to be given
like a life.

The body lying on the wet sand
must leave an impression deeper
than the shallow water
coming to erase it.

May you never recover
from the lightness of my touch.

And they were both right

There is so much violence yet to be done.
He falls into her body
blind because desire makes him blind
deaf and limbless for the same reason.

But what is love?
And is this a question or a statement?

He will be
undone by it, she shudders in jubilation,
and pulls him to her night – like a dress
to be undone.

Love will be made and unmade – naturally,
unnaturally. It will be invoked
like a reason, like a form of life.
It will be forgotten.

What if love is no more than
a tangle of muscles
aching to be untied
by knowing fingers?

What if love is made and nothing else –
asked Narcissus, leaning over the green iris of water.

Nothing else,
cried Echo from the green cochlea of the woods.

And they were both right.
And they were both lonely.

The Sphinx

In the crouching darkness
she gathers.
His body whitely stirs.

Tonight they will attempt
an ecstasy of flattening,
a special mutual herbarium
that only lovers can perform.

At dawn they will be uglier. They will be
hiding in the corners of themselves.
There is only one wisdom at dawn:

searching is better than having.
Despite an entry, the sphinx remains
a monster of history
the visitor cannot share.

Separate in their exhausted possession,
they rise for something else already
as though it will bring them relief.

Poem about Futility

The night begins and ends here,
at the palm tree shaking high above
but never high enough to stab the sky.

You lie on this unfolded arm
which like a stretcher carries you
across the night.
You are followed by a masked procession
of personal silences.

One night, lightning will strike
and grope for you in the black wind.
But now you know he carries you
and he will take you
nowhere in the night.

The palm tree knows the sky will never slip
but it rages in the wind, reaching up,
and that is its feeling.

The procession goes on, and that is yours.
Only the sky travels alone at night
without falling.

Ciphers

Meet the body:
beautiful and ugly.
It has the first and the last word.

At night, it sleeps headless
on pillows of black feathers
and shivers with pleasure and pain.

In the day it sleepwalks
across rooms and cities,
miming its own animation.

Sometimes you hear the sound of it
breaking against a pavement
or an obdurate sky.

How will you ever own it,
the known and unknown corridors
in this temple of disposable time?

How will you ever understand it –
the body is the opposite
of reason?

Tomorrow it will disappear.
Don't try to follow it –
the body has the last word.

Hold it while you can.
Live inside it while you can.
Then someone will collect the ashes.

Still life

On this April day, the trees shed themselves.
The cruelty of seasons
is the only cruelty today.

On this April day something has ended.
Leaves muffle the stridency
of metaphorical mercy killings.

All day you watch a pear on the table.
This pear is all you have today.
You watch it ripen into bruises.
The fruit is here but you can't have it.

If only you could catch that instant
when ripening becomes a bruise,
you could have known once and for all
how we stop loving.

Sleeper

One morning, like a sleeper
you know nothing
other than the dream.
Like a dreamer, you remember nothing
of the dream, now that you're awake
and aching:

your legs ache –
though you've hardly moved
your arms ache –
who have you carried, who have you killed?
your chest aches –
what has weighed upon you?
your eyelids ache –
from seeing too much?

One morning, like a cracked mirror
you reflect the vanishing
of those you knew
through your door
without a house.

You listen to the bats
beat the dawn to shreds
with leather wings.
Shadows disperse outside your window
without curtains or glass.

Have you slept,
or have you tossed and turned
in your roofless house that isn't yours?
Have you loved
have you killed
have you seen?

You have. You have.
You want it again.
But nothing is ever repeated.
Only doubted, only recalled.
How you ache today, sleeper.

No one can touch a laughing man
(for Bruno)

There is a city lacerated by a railway,
a city ending where it should begin.
A city of four rivers and four bridges
for lovers to jump.
A city parallel to life in other places.
On the edge of a continent,
a city pockmarked by absences.

This is where you came from.
This is where you laughed
as the bombs fell and the future darkened.
That's why you laugh still.
You laugh instead of speaking and sleeping,
you've been laughing for years.
No one can touch a laughing man.

The Door

One day you'll see:
you've been knocking on a door
without a house.
You've been waiting, shivering, yelling
words of daring and hope.

One day you'll see:
there is no one on the other side
except as ever, the jubilant ocean
that won't shatter ceramically like a dream
when you and I shatter.

But not yet. Now
you wait outside, watching
the blue arches of mornings
that will break
but are now perfect.

Underneath on tiptoe
pass the faces, speaking to you,
saying 'you', 'you', 'you',
smiling, waving, arriving
in unfailing chronology.

One day you'll doubt your movements,
you will shudder
at the accuracy of your sudden age.
You will ache for slow beauty
to save you from your quick, quick life.

But not yet. Hope
fills the yawn of time.
Blue surrounds you. Now let's say
you see a door and knock,
and wait for someone to hear.

Dismemberment

There is a continent of your memory,
carried by the frivolous tide
of everything that isn't you.
Each morning, you welcome the low tide.
You welcome each sun
that blinds you away from that continent.

But when the storm comes, you remember:
nothing is really quiet.
When the earthquake comes
cracks appear in your mental furniture.
When the moon comes it displays
your passing shadow – a stooped loneliness
so much taller than you.
And yet you're not moving.
No, you're not moving.

In the dark, you listen to the world
shed its silences
and dream of bruising yourself
against a body, or a sharpened soul,
to break with an ice-pick that continent.

When in the dark somebody comes
the continent will float away, dismembered.
And you too will wake up
on a breakaway piece,
alone and naked.
When in the dark somebody comes.

The orchestra on the roof of the city

Always from the highest point
you must watch the roof of the city:
everything happens there
if anything happens at all:

there, the wind reaps its daily harvest
of rotting light;

there, knots of thickening sky
are tied and untied;

there, twilight clouds blossom
from pink to purple to grey to black.

The roof of the city
is the floor of a room
knocked down by wind.
There each night

if you listen through velvety
curtains of sleep
are played the wind's symphonies
by an orchestra you must never see.

Mirages

Waking up in the same skin isn't enough.
You need more and more evidence
of who it is that
wakes up in the same skin.

But what evidence?
Reality is unreliable: a whirlwind
of dust that appears
and disappears every day.

Your thirst stretches out its white dunes.

Every day in the dust
you distinguish

not islands but their darkness
heaped on the polished mirror of a sea.

Not doors but their shadows
slammed in the house of wind.

Not lighthouses but their half-second SOS
in red, green and yellow.

Not language but languages.

Not your hand closing a curtain
but a hand.

And the day is over,
not wiser than the night in which
you waited for something
that came and wasn't what you'd waited for.

Preparation for the big emptiness

Smudges of moon in the morning –
fingerprints of the moon-eaters

A new core gathers for the evening
to be plucked and crumbled by other hands

Sometimes, there is blue in between
Sometimes, there is no one

You must prepare for the big
emptiness to come

It has come

When it comes
you must spread yourself thinly,
transparently,
to fill what can't be filled

It has come

Unlike the moon you must do it
without breaking

Marseille

Out in the steep afternoon
masts rattle in the wind.
Arab children rub their raw knees.
Their fathers sell used laces,
handless watches, legless pants.
Their mothers rock in shuttered rooms
up where the gulls begin their fall
and everybody's washing flaps high
in the sky making a patchwork
of bleeding colours.

The whore of memory

To wake up is to be the whore of waking up –
in yet another town, in yet another
native tongue.

To wake up is to be the whore of waking up,
to cut off the white hands
of sleep's pantomime,
to look down at the troubled green
of an untroubled sea,
to hear the day's stranger
breathe inside you.
Where are you?

Don't strain your memory for an answer.
Tomorrow you'll forget.
You are the whore of memory.

Oyster

Inexplicable anger: I can't.
Can't be, can't have, can't go.

Distance is the subtle terror
of your longing. Longing is greed.
Your greed like a prey
seeks a distant hunter.

Stop. Consider
the landscape of your life:
clusters of moments touching each other
with phantom limbs.

Phantom limbs
and the trunk of being here: this
is the animal
you have become.

Crawl towards the hard blue and the crumbling white.
You'll get what you are seeking:
not simply colours but colours
sharpened into creatures by rotting light.

Roll like the red ball of the sun
all the way to where
you'll be opened like an oyster
by the claws of something stronger

shrieking: I can never
have the world.

A city of pierced amphorae

You can say that everything
is circumstantial clutter now.
You swim across the Mediterranean
and sprawl on hot white rock.
You swim back too.
Naturally, you'll never drown
because you have no sense of the absurd.

Until the summer day is over
and the islands float away,
promising no definite return.
Until the night stretches infinitely.
Until tomorrow rises like a carved portal
in all its vertical intricacy.

You bang the knocker, someone hears,
someone rushes to open
but has no hands.
You listen to each other breathe
as if to say: nothing's lost,
but nothing's left on this side.
And so until the answer rises.
Slow and dark, a tidal wave.

You've been waiting for the tidal wave,
you the midnight city of pierced amphorae.
You are submersed and happy.
To be so loved by water,
you must be perfectly quiet.
You must die.

ALL ROADS LEAD TO THE SEA

young poems from the end of the world

FROM *The immigrant cycle*

Coming to paradise

We came and found paradise but something
was missing in the water, in the sky,
in the movement of hands
that couldn't embrace or punish

Our children have the large
moist eyes of wounded deer
but must betray no sign of weakness
they must be winners or nothing

Our children know all the songs
all the shows all the jokes
they try to learn the memories too
our children are like the rest

It's a sign of fluency to dream in a language
but we dream wide-awake
we think about our dreams
in broken silences

We stand alone and stubborn
we spend years looking for a crack
in the neighbours' wall
but only find a key

We came looking for paradise and paradise
we found, but it wasn't enough
so we wept and talked about leaving
and never left.

Security

After the long day
My father locks the doors
The windows
The blinds on the windows
He locks out the voice of the wind
The question of yesterday

My mother turns off every light
In every room, in every cupboard
She turns off the TV
The red light of the heart flashing
The last star
In this forever foreign sky

And carefully they lie in bed
Listening to the sound
Of growing children

Razor salesman

Olive skinned and unshaven behind the wheel
the salesman is weary,
he balances on the verge of speaking
lights a cigarette
and doesn't say much until
the sun has crawled to the other side
of the globe where
my cousins and brothers
are cutting each other's throats

he hates his life of a salesman
going from door to door, town to town
alone in this car packed
with boxes of razors
spinning out the same tale,
driving until there's nowhere let to go
under the bloody sun,
until all the razors are sold
and all the wars silenced
and then, then maybe
he can go home

My father climbing to the stars

In the strangest dream my father –
a compressed, stubborn angel –
climbs the cabbage tree outside

In the strangest dream my father
always falls interminably
like a curled leaf
through the seasons of my life

When I'm awake
my father climbs
the cabbage tree outside

severing the highest leaves
making way for the light
because I suffer from darkness

But now the neighbours can see me
and my father weaves a fence
with the severed cabbage-leaves

At night, when I sit by the window
sad under the southern sky
my father is still
climbing some stairway, my father

will rearrange the stars
in a pattern
less dissonant to my eyes

My mother's plants

My mother brings the strangest plants,
she gives them to me
then she waters them
because she knows I will forget.

Sometimes I wait in the big house
behind closed curtains
because I am afraid
I touch a door-knob – it comes off.
I stroke a loaf of bread –
it feels like a broken spine.
I turn on the heater –
a carpet burns to ashes.
I water the plants –
they die instantly.

I wait and fear the worst –
my mother lying in a furrow
somewhere in the white
fields of light
facing a sky so dark
that nobody can see it.

Song of the Stranger

There is such a thing as excessive peace
it creeps up on the stranger like fog
There is a place where

war is in the form of small eruptions
of rain poetry on a Sunday afternoon

where taking a breath can last
up to a lifetime

where the sky looks the stranger
in the eye with no fear

where fern has the intricate
simplicity of symbol

where a herd of clouds grazing on thunder
follows the stranger

all the way to the middle of the ocean
but never beyond

* * *

Sick of the ocean

In the winter of our youth
the ocean was cold
and in the summer of our later years too.
We are sick of seeing the ocean
of hearing the ocean
tasting its blood
metallic and cruel.
But here, there is no other season,
there is only the ocean
carrying unwanted Sundays
like seagulls travelling on slow waves
towards the cold beaches of our palms
where nothing grows
where we draw with sticks
our long names and small hearts
where everything including the future
is neatly washed out
on the next day.

Insularity

Each day, the house contains you.
The shower cap contains your head.
The plate contains your dinner.

Outside is the terror of leaving,
The vertigo of pavements,
The inquisition of the sky.

Inside, the corners shelter you
from the centre of rooms,
the walls soothe you
from the abrasion of carpets.

But in your coat you wriggle
like a minotaur inside a labyrinth:
not looking for the way out
but hungry – and alone.

All roads lead to the sea

All roads lead to the sea, says the driver
and talks to a passenger about living in Roxburgh,
about the weather, taxes and his daughter
who studies home science.

We drive through landscapes
frozen in the wind
like metaphors for timid minds

through empty towns called Roxburgh
knowing nothing but the sea
and how to die.

Above the hills' broken shadows
the sun begins to fall and we are almost
there – all roads lead to the sea.

BV - #0020 - 260320 - C0 - 216/138/6 - PB - 9781852246174